W9-BNT-908

Cats Are Better than Men

Cats Are Better than Men

Beverly Guhl

Doubleday

New York
London
Toronto
Sydney
Auckland

PUBLISHED BY DOUBLEDAY
a division of Bantam Doubleday Dell Publishing Group, Inc.
1540 Broadway, New York, New York 10036

MAIN STREET BOOKS, DOUBLEDAY, and the portrayal of a building with a tree
are trademarks of Doubleday, a division of Bantam
Doubleday Dell Publishing Group, Inc.

Book design by Jennifer Ann Daddio

Library of Congress Cataloging-in-Publication Data

Guhl, Beverly, 1952-
Cats are better than men / Beverly Guhl.
p. cm.
1. Cats--Humor. I. Title.
PN6231.C23G84 1994
818' .5402--dc20 93-40092
CIP

ISBN 0-385-47169-6
Copyright © 1994 by Beverly Guhl
All Rights Reserved
Printed in the United States of America
July 1994
First Edition
10 9 8 7 6 5 4 3 2 1

TO CATS AND MEN EVERYWHERE,
WITHOUT WHOM THIS BOOK COULD NOT HAVE BEEN WRITTEN

Cats Are Better than Men

They never complain about your weight.

oh boy! snack time AGAIN!!

They never accuse you of being too emotional.

Is dis my itty bitty Kitty? Es it is! It IS my itty bitty Kitty!! Oooooh, Mummy wuvs her itty bitty...

They can show their emotions.

They take an interest in your work.

They never leave the seat up.

They don't care how much money you spend.

They don't use up all the hot water.

They don't need to see a shrink.

Smart Women, Idiotic Choicee
Carl Jung
Freudian Dating Dos 'ts
Women Who Love Too Darn Much
The Codependency Hoax
You're OK, They're Crazy
Cats Are Better than Men
The 12 Steps, 24 Hops and 43 Jumps Program
Men Who Hate Women and the Women Who Hate Them Back
The Road More Traveled

They always let you know when
they plan to go out.

They're eager to please you.

They never have other plans.

They heartily approve of your
taste in furnishings.

They don't complain about work
or their boss.

They don't talk about themselves.

They're kissable, and there's
no beard burn.

They think you look just fine
without makeup.

They don't require closet space.

They don't cheat on you.

They listen to your problems.

They never try to make you
feel guilty.

CHOCOLATES

They don't care what you wear to bed.

They don't eat up all the food
in the fridge.

Cat Chows
WATER
CHOW

They never say they'll call
then never call.

They LOVE yard work.

They like to snuggle all night long.

They never break dates at
the last minute.

They're never late for dinner.

Whirrrrrr
CATCH
CHOW

Their grooming habits are never in question.

They never complain about your cooking.

...or your friends...

...or your new hairdo.

Hair

They don't work weekends.

They never ask to borrow money.

They LOVE leftovers.

They think you look wonderful
in the morning.

They can take care of themselves
when you go out.

CHO
WAIT

They don't leave smelly socks
all over the house.

They never make you feel stupid.

They're always bringing you gifts.

They don't hide behind a newspaper.

They love your fuzzy terry bathrobe as much as you do.

They don't care if you don't shave your legs for days or weeks.

They LOVE your mother.

They have impeccable table manners.

WATER
CHOW

They're never on the phone.

They like romance novels, too.

They never complain about your housekeeping.

They don't watch sports on TV.

CLICK

They love dinner parties.

What a cute cat!
How affectionate!
Isn't this the sweetest Kitty?!!
Is it ok to give the cat some salmon?

They don't hog the covers or snore.

About the Author

Beverly Guhl has designed and marketed everything from greeting cards and stationery to decorative magnets, record albums, and mugs. She has also written and illustrated two previous books: *Purrfect Parenting* and *Teenage Years–A Parent's Survival Guide*. The mother of two college-age children and one cat, she lives in Austin, Texas, where she is Director of Graphics for the Texas Department of Protective and Regulatory Services. Although a staunch supporter of human rights and gender equality, she says she would probably vote for a cat if one ran for office.